The King's Magic Cloaks

by Judith Queripel
Arranged and Edited by Alison Hedger

A musical play for any time of the year with seven songs, optional improvised music, percussion and dance

Duration approx. 30 mins.

For children 4 to 9 years and those with learning difficulties
Key Stage 1 and lower 2 Special Education Units

TEACHER'S BOOK
Music, production notes and play included.

"The King's Magic Cloaks is dedicated to the very special children of Bracken Hill School, Kirkby in Ashfield, Notts with whom I have had so much fun.

Pupils of all ages took part in our production.
The youngest, 3 to 7 year olds were the soldiers, the 8 to 12 years were the king's child subjects and the 13 to 17 year olds were the adults of the kingdom. The more able from each group took the speaking parts.

The message of the play is universal and can be understood at many different levels. The musical is therefore appropriate not only for children in special education, but also for those in mainstream Infant and Junior schools."
Judith Queripel

MUSIC

Song 1 Our Castle
Optional improvised music depicting whistling wind
Song 2 The Salesmen's Song
Song 3 A Good Job Done
Song 4 He's Mean
Party Jig
Song 5 Jelly and Ice Cream (possible 2 part round)
Song 6 There's A Song
Children's solo favourite nursery rhymes
Song 7 Sing This Song (optional tuned percussion or recorder)

A matching tape cassette of the music for rehearsals and performances is available, Order No. GA10944, side A with vocals included, side B with vocals omitted.

A division of Chester Music Limited
8/9 Frith Street, London W1V 5TZ

Order No. GA10931
ISBN0-7119-4163-7

CAST LIST

Speaking Parts

NARRATOR(S)
ONE OR TWO SOLDIERS
SALESMAN ONE } who could sing solo in Song 3
SALESMAN TWO
QUEEN
PRINCE
PRINCESS
THREE SUBJECTS who could be children, young ladies or young men.

Other Parts

SOLDIERS	who march and salute, and take and pass back various items.
THE KING'S SUBJECTS	who sing and dance, and provide sounds of happy laughter. Individuals pass over and receive back again their own treasured possessions.
MUSICIANS	who provide improvised percussion music depicting the whistling wind.
SOLO SINGERS	who perform their favourite nursery rhyme for the king.

NARRATION AND PLAY PARTS

The narration carries the story and is best read by an adult or perhaps older children if using THE KING'S MAGIC CLOAKS in a mainstream school. The characters are given a prompt in the script, eg "The king said". The play parts are simple and can be improvised successfully if the characters are unable to remember word for word what to say.

Two places in the script are marked with an asterisk *. On page 8 the soldiers take from the subjects their treasured possessions and give them to the greedy king. On page 11 the possessions are taken from the king and passed back by the soldiers to their rightful owners. This can be elaborated upon or passed over quickly. In the original production each child and possession were named by the narrator as this acted as a prompt. It was hard to pass over some items (and took quite a little time!) but much joy was had in getting one's own things back again!

SCENERY

This is not necessary, however a colourful backdrop or painted inside walls of the castle could be effective.

COSTUMES

These are naturally suggested by the characters. THE KING'S MAGIC CLOAKS provides an excellent opportunity for dressing up. Parents and friends will no doubt be pleased to oblige with items of clothing. The soldiers look visually best in bright red.

PROPS

2 Magic Cloaks (1 shiny and new 1 old and tatty)	these are central to the play and it is imagined that every member of the cast will want to put them on at some stage!
Well-loved Possessions (toys, objects, etc.)	see opposite page for paragraph explaining two places marked ★ in the script.

MUSIC

The songs are melodious and appeal to all children regardless of learning abilities. Chord symbols are provided for electronic keyboard or guitar. A cassette tape of the music is obtainable from the publishers.

The improvised whistling wind music can be rehearsed or spontaneous and may provide an opportunity to use skills already discovered in class music. Alison Hedger gives ideas for this should you need them. They are to be found on page 28.

The collective playing of percussion instruments to the songs should be positive and great fun!

THE KING'S MAGIC CLOAKS provides a good moment for eager singers to share their solo singing. Nursery rhymes will be recognised whatever the ability of the soloist and will be a heart-winning moment in the production.

A simple counter melody for song 7 for recorder or tuned percussion has been given should you wish to use it. Song 5 can be sung as a two-part round if desired.

DANCE

As uninhibited as possible.

THE KING'S MAGIC CLOAKS

Narrator A long time ago in a far off land there stood a castle. It was a beautiful castle with pointed towers and smart soldiers to guard it.

SONG 1 OUR CASTLE

1\. Our castle is a fine old building,
It stands on the highest ground.
The walls are thick and made of stone,
And the soldiers go marching round and round,
And the soldiers go marching round.

Chorus It looks alright on the outside,
But things aren't what they seem.
For you will find if you go inside
That it's very cold when the wind blows,
It's very cold when the wind blows.
It's very cold in the wind.

2\. Our castle is a fine old building,
It stands on the highest ground.
The windows are tall and have no glass,
So the wind whistles round and round and round,
So the wind whistles round and round.

Chorus It looks alright …

(*OPTIONAL IMPROVISED MUSIC to DESCRIBE THE WHISTLING WIND see page 28*)

Narrator Inside the cold draughty castle lived a king with his queen, the prince and princess. Everyone loved the queen for she was beautiful and kind. Everyone loved the prince and princess for they were always happy and their laughter could be heard throughout the land. Everyone loved the king because he had always been a naturally generous man. The royal family may have been cold in their castle but they were happy, and so were all the people in the land.

Then one day something happened that changed everything. Some double glazing salesmen came to visit the king. They went to find a soldier who took them to the king. The soldier said,

Soldier Your majesty, there are two people to see you.

SONG 2 THE SALESMEN'S SONG

1. When the double glazing salesmen come
You're always sure to be
Getting ready to go out
Or sitting down to tea.

Chorus But the king didn't mind,
He really didn't mind.
He didn't mind a bit.
For it was a dream of his to find
Some windows that would fit.
Some windows that would fit.

2. When the double glazing salesmen come
And knock upon your door,
You'll be in the middle of a job.
Of that be sure.

Chorus But the king …

3. When the double glazing salesmen come
They often know your name.
When you try to shut the door
They stand there just the same.

Chorus But the king …

Narrator Salesman one said to the king,

Salesman One Your majesty, this castle has been chosen to try out our new windproof double glazing.

Salesman Two If you let us fit the windows we will give you two free magic cloaks.

Narrator The king who was in the middle of his tea, jumped up with delight and said,

King Oh yes! What a marvellous offer! You can start the work right away, but mind you do a good job.

SONG 3 A GOOD JOB DONE

1. The windows in the castle are such a funny shape.
But fitting them is really lots of fun.
The king seems to think we're getting on alright,
So it soon will be a good job done, you'll see.
It soon will be a good job done.

Chorus Oh! Our special double glazing,
Our special double glazing
Keeps out the wind but lets in all the sun.
(*sing Chorus twice*)

2. There are so many windows we cannot count them all.
Enough to keep the workers on the run.
The king seems to think we're getting on alright,
So it soon will be a good job done, you'll see.
It soon will be a good job done.

Chorus Oh! Our special double glazing …

3. Be careful with the windows, be careful not to fall.
Be careful not to break a single one.
The king seems to think we're getting on alright,
So it soon will be a good job done, you'll see.
It soon will be a good job done.

Chorus Oh! Our special double glazing …

Narrator At last all the windows were fitted. The king was pleased because his castle was now warm and cosy. He called the two salesmen to him and said,

King Here is your money.

Salesman One Here are your two magic cloaks.

Salesman Two Be sure to wear one of them every day.

Narrator The king was very pleased and gladly took the two cloaks.

Narrator Now, one of the cloaks was beautiful, colourful and very shiny. The other one was old, dull and ragged. So when the king woke up next morning, he naturally put on his lovely shiny cloak. How splendid he looked in it! He went straight off to show everyone in the castle how fine he looked. But as the king gloried in his appearance something awful was happening to him. He began to feel greedy and started to wish for things that belonged to other people. As the days passed, he continued to wear his shiny cloak and thought what a fine figure of a man he was. But he was getting greedier and meaner as time went on. He took things that were not his and filled the castle with things that he had taken. He was now a truly greedy and mean man.

SONG 4 HE'S MEAN

Chorus

He's mean, he's mean,
He's the meanest king you have ever seen.
He's mean, he's mean,
He's the meanest there's ever been.

1. He takes what he likes, our toys and our bikes.
He's as mean as mean can be.
He's mean, he's mean,
He's the meanest there's ever been.

Chorus He's mean ...

2. He takes what he sees, our plants and our trees.
He's as mean as mean can be.
He's mean, he's mean,
He's the meanest there's ever been.

Chorus He's mean ...

3. He takes what he can, our pots and our pans.
He's as mean as mean can be.
He's mean, he's mean,
He's the meanest there's ever been.

Narrator As soon as the king saw something he wanted, he sent soldiers to get it for him.

*

Nobody argued because you can't say "no" to a king! But everyone was very unhappy. However, nobody was as unhappy and miserable as the king himself!

Then one morning the queen said to him,

Queen Why don't you put on your other cloak today, dear?

Narrator The prince said,

Prince Go on Dad, you haven't tried it on yet.

Narrator The princess said,

Princess Please put the other cloak on, it might make you feel better.

Narrator But the king said,

King What! Put on that ragged old thing? Never. I am the king. I can only wear beautiful clothes.

Narrator And so the king went on wearing the shiny cloak, and he got meaner and meaner, and greedier and greedier, and more and more unhappy.

Whenever the king heard laughter, he shut himself away and thought the meanest thoughts he could. Why should anyone be happy when he was so miserable?

Now, the prince and princess liked people to be happy, so they decided to hold a party. They invited everyone in the land, as everyone needed cheering up. Perhaps their father would come and then feel better. So the prince said to the king,

Prince Please come to our party.

Narrator And the princess said,

Princess Forget all your troubles and be happy.

Narrator The party took place, and the castle was filled with music and the sound of happy laughter.

PARTY JIG MUSIC

Dancing by entire cast, except the grumpy king.

Narrator The king was not pleased, and he said,

King Go away. You are much too happy.

Narrator The king returned to his room to think of the meanest thing he could do. But the prince and princess loved their father and did not give up. They decided to hold a big feast. Surely the king would enjoy that, and join in when he saw all the lovely food. So they again invited everyone to the castle. The prince said to the king,

Prince Please come to our feast.

Narrator And the princess said,

Princess Forget all your troubles and be happy.

Narrator The feast took place, and the castle was filled with gorgeous food and the sound of happy laughter.

SONG 5 JELLY AND ICE CREAM

Jelly and ice cream, jelly and ice cream,
Biscuits and cakes and lovely buns.

Big sausage rolls and our favourite crisps. Yes!
Plenty for everyone.

Narrator The king still was not pleased, and he said,

King Go away. You are all much too happy.

Narrator The king again returned to his room to think of the meanest thing he could. But the prince and princess loved their father and did not give up. They decided to hold a concert. Surely the king would enjoy that, and feel a lot better this time. So again they invited everyone to the castle. The prince said to the king,

Prince Please come to our concert.

Narrator The princess said,

Princess Forget all your troubles and be happy.

Narrator The concert took place, and the castle was filled with the the sound of everyone singing.

SONG 6 THERE'S A SONG

1. There's a song we can sing together.
There's a song we can sing alone.
However you feel, whether blue skies or grey,
There's a song for everyday.

2. (*as above, with altered words for 3rd line*)
Wherever you are, at your home or away,

3. Whatever you do, either at work or play,

Narrator At first the king was crosser than ever. Then he sat down and began to listen.

(*At this point, individual children come forward and sing their best-loved nursery rhymes. The narrator introduces each soloist by name.*)

When the songs had finished the king put his head in his hands and began to cry. One child (*young lady, or young gentleman*) said,

Child One Poor king. Whatever is the matter?

Narrator A second child said,

Child Two Poor king. Why are you crying?

Narrator A third child said,

Child Three Poor king. We wanted to make you happy not sad.

Narrator The king said,

King How can I be happy when I cannot even enjoy the sound of sweet music? I have everything I could wish for, but I am not happy. I wish I was happy like you.

Narrator Everyone went home feeling rather sad. The king went to his room and took off his shiny cloak. The next morning the king still felt miserable and was crying to himself. His eyes were all red and puffy from the tears and he couldn't see properly. He put on the ragged cloak instead of the shiny one.

Suddenly, he felt a whole lot better!

He looked around at all the things he had taken from other people and felt ashamed, and said,

King I don't need these things. I must give them back.

Narrator The king called his soldiers and told them to get everyone back to the castle. Back came everybody and the king returned all the things he had taken away.

It took a very long time to do this, but the soldiers did not stop until every single thing was back to its rightful owner.

The king was feeling like he used to, and was now getting quite happy! He wanted to give the biggest and best party ever. He said,

King Let's dance and sing.

Narrator Everyone shouted with glee,

All Yes! Let's dance and sing.

SONG 7 SING THIS SONG

Sing this song and dance about,
Play your instruments and shout.
Clap your hands and tap your feet,
Sway around and feel the beat.
Sway around and feel the beat.

(*The king joins in and enjoys all the fun*)

Narrator The king was singing and dancing like everyone else. One child said,

Child One Look! The king is singing.

Narrator A second child said,

Child Two Three cheers for our king.

Narrator A third child said,

Child Three Hip, hip

All HOORAY!

Child Three Hip, hip

All HOORAY!

Child Three Hip, hip

All HOOOO – RAY!!

Narrator The king leapt in the air for joy and said,

King I can enjoy myself again. I can sing. I can dance.

Narrator The king wished he had worn the ragged cloak sooner. He never ever wanted to put the shiny one on again.

Now, there's a moral to this tale
As I am sure you'll see.
Not everything attractive,
Is what it seems to be.

The castle strong and beautiful
Inside was cold it seems.
The shiny cloak made the king
Become greedy, sad and mean.

But when he wore the ragged one
And forgot about his pride,
He stopped his unkind actions
And felt differently inside.

For no one is so important
That they can ever say,
"I must have the best,
Must always have MY way."

That's not the way to happiness,
As you will surely find.
It is the ordinary simple things
That bring joy and peace of mind.

REPEAT SONG 7 SING THIS SONG

(During the following, the characters take their bows to cheers from the rest of the cast)

Narrator	Hooray for the beautiful castle, And the soldiers who marched around. Hooray for the window salesmen Whose cloaks were to astound.	 (*march and salute*) (*deep bow*)
	Hooray for the two magic cloaks To choose to wear each day. Hooray for the queen so calm and kind Who smiled, come what may.	(*hold up cloaks*) (*curtsy*)
	Hooray for the prince and princess, Always trying to find A way to make the king become Happy, good and kind.	 (*bow and curtsy*)
	Hooray for the king, who in the end Put right the wrong he'd done. Hooray for all who've danced, and sung. Hooray for everyone!	 (*bow*)
All	HOOO - RAY !!	

FINAL REPEAT OF SONG 7 SING THIS SONG

THE END

SONG ONE
OUR CASTLE

(During this song the soldiers could march and salute)

Cue: ... smart soldiers to guard it.

Chorus
D7
G
G
G/F#
sol - diers go march - ing round.
wind whis - tles round and round.
It looks al - right on the
Am7
G
Am7
D
G
G/F#
out - side, but things aren't what they seem. For you will find if you
Am7
D7
G
G/F#
C
G
go in - side that it's ve - ry cold when the wind blows, it's
C
G
Am7
G
D7
G
ve - ry cold when the wind blows. It's ve - ry cold in the wind.

SONG TWO
THE SALESMEN'S SONG

Cue: … there are two people to see you.

Chorus
D Bm7 Gmaj7 Em7 A D Em7
king did - n't mind, he real - ly did - n't mind. He did - n't mind a
A G D Em7 A7
bit. For it was a dream of his to find some
Em7add9 Em7 A A7 D A7
win - dows that would fit. Some win - dows that would
To repeat
D Bm A7 D
fit.
2. When the
3. When the
Final time
D
fit.

SONG THREE
A GOOD JOB DONE

Cue: … but mind you do a good job.

C
Fm
B♭m
C
Fm
C
Fm
E♭
right, so it soon will be a good job done, you'll see. It

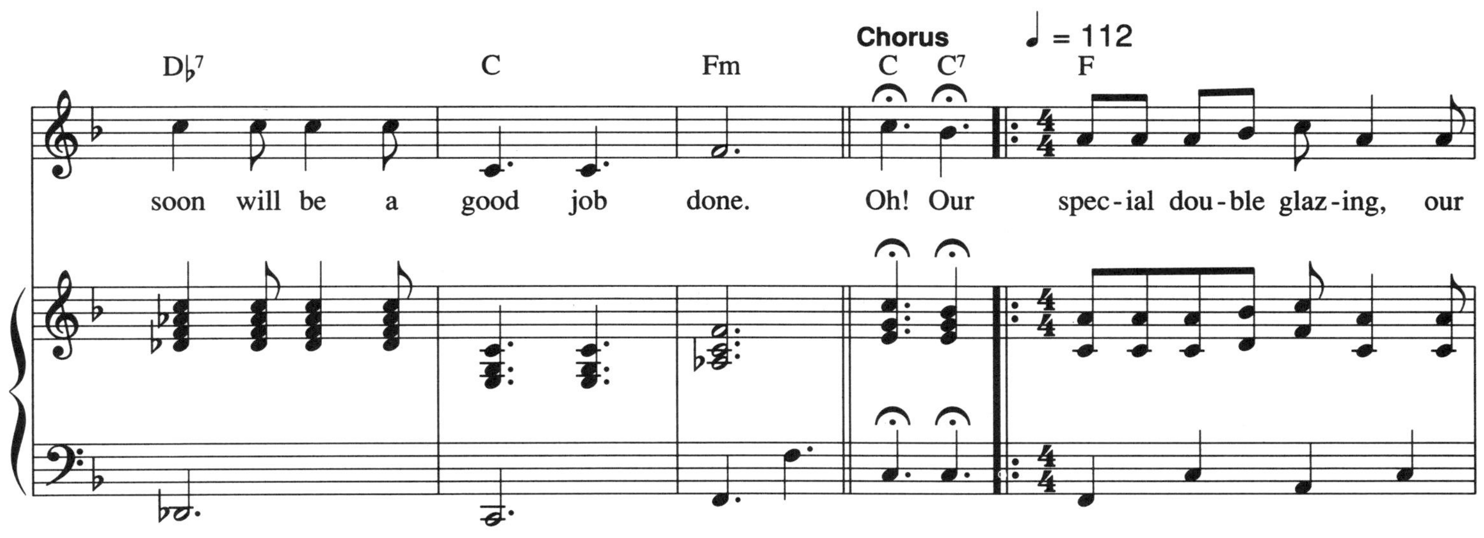
Chorus
♩ = 112
D♭7
C
Fm
C
C7
F
soon will be a good job done. Oh! Our spec-ial dou-ble glaz-ing, our

1st time
2nd time
B♭
C/B♭
B♭
C
C7
F
C
C7
F
Fine
spec-ial dou-ble glaz-ing keeps out the wind but lets in all the sun. Oh! Our sun.

SONG FOUR
HE'S MEAN

Cue: He was now a truly greedy and mean man.

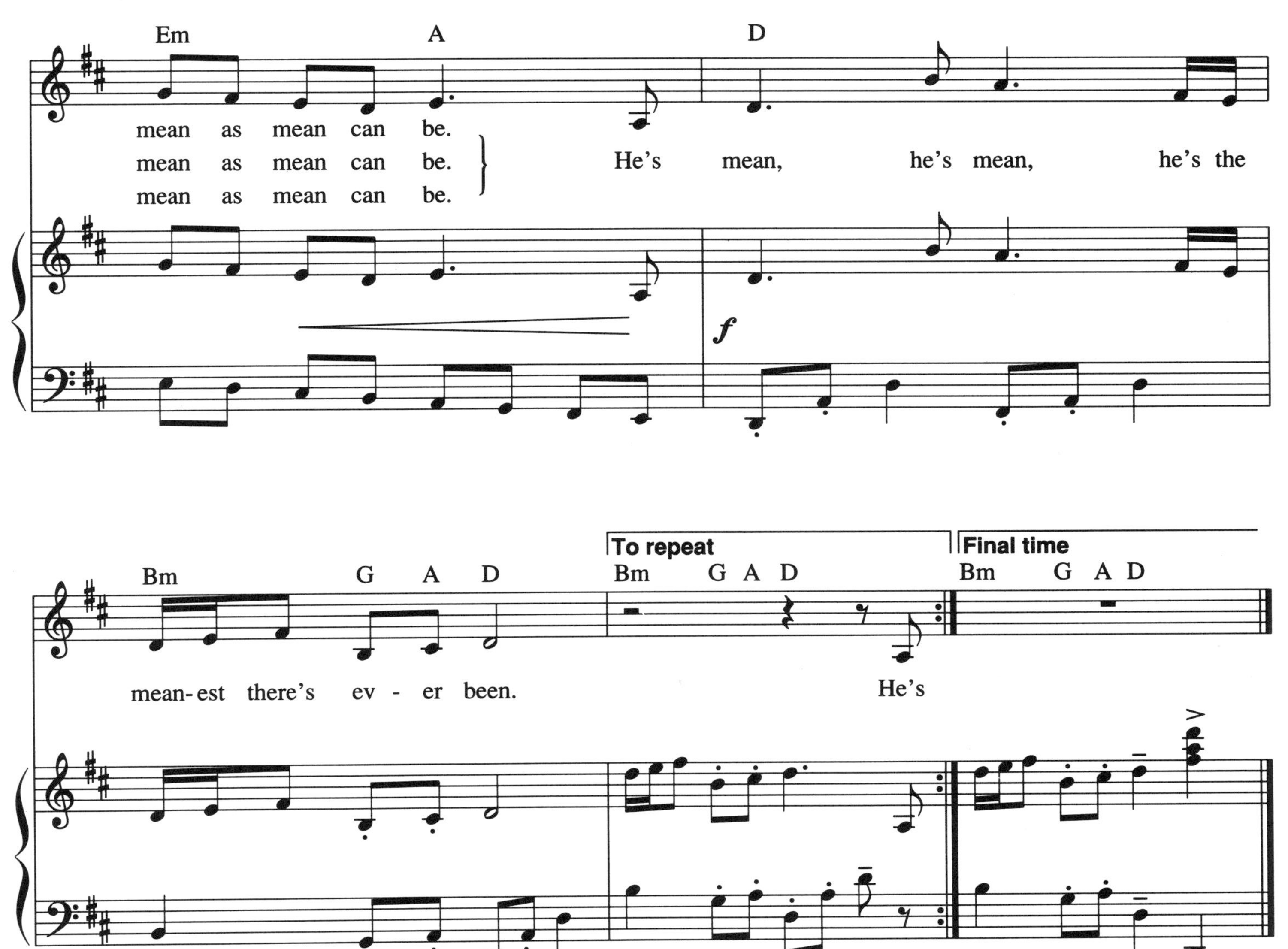
Em A D
mean as mean can be.
mean as mean can be. He's mean, he's mean, he's the
mean as mean can be.
f
Bm G A D
mean-est there's ev - er been.
To repeat
Bm G A D
He's
Final time
Bm G A D

PARTY JIG

Music for dancing

Cue: … and the castle was filled with music and the sound of happy laughter.

SONG FIVE
JELLY AND ICE CREAM

Can be sung as a two-part round.

Cue: ... gorgeous food and the sound of happy laughter.

* Entry point for part 2

SONG SIX
THERE'S A SONG

Cue: … the sound of everyone singing.

D
Bm
G
D
A7
blue skies or grey,
home or a - way,
at work or play,
there's a song for ev - ery -

To repeat
Final time
D
A7
D
day.
2.
3.
There's a
day.

SONG SEVEN
SING THIS SONG

Assorted percussion instruments play along in time with the music.

Hand claps = 2 per bar

Cue: 1) Yes! Let's dance and sing.

2) ...bring joy and peace of mind.

3) HOOO-RAY!!

Repeat song as many times as desired.

IDEAS FOR THE OPTIONAL IMPROVISED MUSIC FOR THE WIND

See page 4

Discuss with children the type of sound the wind makes as it passes over and through things. Talk about the sound that is made as the wind passes over trees and how the sound differs when the wind hits a building and blows through windows, doors, alley ways and around chimneys. What effect does the wind have on ill-fitting windows and doors? What can a wild wind do to unsecured objects? What is a draught?

Having thought about the above, "discover" types of vocal sounds which will make a sound picture of the wind. eg

a) suck in air and blow out heavily
b) a shhhhhh sound
c) a whoooo sound through pursed lips
d) hiss through teeth
e) whistle

Think of everyday objects which could depict the sound of the wind. eg

a) flapping pieces of paper
b) blowing across bottle tops

Use percussion instruments to extend the sound picture. eg

a) run beaters lightly over the bars of glockenspiels, xylophones and metallophones
b) use a Swanee Whistle, making quivering rises and falls
c) metal brushes for swishing noises

Each child chooses or is delegated a particular sound colour and should be aware of all the other participants. To make the sound picture plausible, there should be a rise and fall in pitch and loudness. Avoid everyone blasting forth at full strength all at once! A leader could conduct the music using obvious hand and arm signals, or if the musicians are competent, and few in number, the sound picture could be spontaneous. It would prove very useful to tape record the music before your performance, so that the children can critically analyse their efforts, so giving them an opportunity to improve their music and to make perhaps a more realistic sound!

If time allows the above work can be extended by using percussion instruments to add some humour to the sound picture. eg

a) drums and cymbols for the blowing over of a royal dustbin!
b) shakers and rattles for the rattling of window and door frames.

The above unit of work provides a good opportunity to begin work on graphic score writing, using simple symbols such as:

Printed and bound in Great Britain by
Caligraving Limited Thetford Norfolk